NEW VANGUARD 209

FRENCH TANKS OF WORLD WAR II (1)

Infantry and Battle Tanks

STEVEN J. ZALOGA   ILLUSTRATED BY IAN PALMER

First published in Great Britain in 2014 by Osprey Publishing,
PO Box 883, Oxford, OX1 9PL, UK
PO Box 3985, New York, NY 10185-3985, USA
E-mail: info@ospreypublishing.com

Osprey Publishing is part of the Osprey Group

A CIP catalog record for this book is available from the British Library

Print ISBN: 978 1 78200 389 2
PDF e-book ISBN: 978 1 4728 0775 5
EPUB e-book ISBN: 978 1 4728 0776 2

Index by Zoe Ross
Typeset in Sabon and Myriad Pro
Originated by PDQ Media, Bungay, UK
Printed in China through Worldprint Ltd.

14 15 16 17 18   10 9 8 7 6 5 4 3 2 1

www.ospreypublishing.com

Osprey Publishing is supporting the Woodland Trust, the UK's leading
woodland conservation charity, by funding the dedication of trees.

GLOSSARY

AMX	Atelier de construction d'Issy-les-Moulineaux
APX	Ateliers de construction de Puteaux
APX-R	Turret designed by APX and cast at Atelier de Rueil (ARL)
ARL	Atelier de Rueil
BCC	Bataillon de chars de combat (tank battalion)
BCP	Bataillon de chasseurs portés (mechanized infantry battalion)
CACC	Compagnie autonome de chars de combat (separate tank company)
DCr	Division cuirassée (armored division)
DLM	Division légère mécanique (light mechanized division)
FCM	Forges et Chantier de la Méditerranée
FAMH	Forges et Acieres de la Marine et d'Homécourt
FF	Franc française (French franc)
Mle.	Abbreviation for Modèle (Model)
RCA	Régiment de chasseurs d'Afrique
RCC	Régiment de chars de combat (tank regiment)
SEAM	Société d'études et d'applications mécaniques
STCC	Section téchnique de chars de combat
TRC	Tracteur de ravitaillement pour chars (tank resupply vehicle)

EDITOR'S NOTE

For ease of comparison please refer to the following conversion table:

1 mile = 1.6km
1yd = 0.9m
1ft = 0.3m
1in = 2.54cm/25.4mm
1 gallon (Imperial) = 4.5 litres
1lb = 0.45kg

CONTENTS

FRENCH TANKS OF WORLD WAR II (1)
INFANTRY AND BATTLE TANKS

THE LEGACY TANK: RENAULT FT

The Renault FT was modernized in the mid-1930s by refitting the turret with the Reibel 7.5mm machine gun in a new mount, as seen on the tank to the right. The tank on the left is a standard Char Canon, armed with the 37 SA18. (NARA)

In the wake of World War I, the French army demobilized much of its tank force.[1] The obsolete Schneider CA and Saint-Chamond tanks were mothballed and eventually scrapped. The hundred newly arrived British Mark V* heavy tanks remained in service until 1929–30. The modern Char Léger Renault FT became the basis for the postwar French tank force.

During the interwar years, the French tank force was dominated by the legacy of the Renault FT tank. As of the armistice day of November 11, 1918,

---

1   Steven Zaloga, *French Tanks of World War I*, Osprey New Vanguard 173, 2010.

The Renault FT remained in service through 1940 and continued to see combat in France's colonies in the years after. This is a Renault FT Char Canon, built by Delaunay-Belleville in one of the postwar batches, which took part in the fighting against the US Army in Morocco in November 1942 during the Operation *Torch* landings. (NARA)

a total of 3,187 Renault FT tanks had been delivered, of which 2,720 had been received by the army, 220 not yet delivered, and 530 exported, mainly to the American Expeditionary Force (514). Total wartime casualties had been 440 tanks. Production of the Renault FT continued at several of the factories after the armistice to fulfill existing contracts. In total, some 4,517 were manufactured, including the major variants such as the TSF radio tank (100 delivered), and the Char Canon de 75S (40 delivered). As of December 1921, the French army counted some 3,588 Renault FT ready for mobilization, and at the time of the occupation of the Rhineland there were still nine tank regiments, each with three battalions of 72 tanks each. A report at the end of 1934 indicated that 3,499 were still ready for mobilization. Many Renault FT tanks were exported in the interwar years and it became the seed of many tank forces around the world, including the USA, Russia, Poland, and China.

With such a large inventory on hand, there was very little incentive for further production of infantry tanks through the 1920s. Organizational changes in the French army undermined much enthusiasm for heavy expenditures on new tanks. In 1914–18, tanks had been fostered by the Artillerie d'Assaut under Gén Jean-Baptiste Estienne. This special branch was dissolved in May 1920 and the tanks handed over to a small tank section (STCC: *section téchnique de chars de combat*) within the infantry department. Gén Estienne remained as the tank inspector through 1930, and continued to foster new tank concepts, albeit with little enthusiasm from the infantry. The demilitarization of the German army after the Treaty of Versailles removed France's most obvious foreign threat, further undermining any rationale for modernization of the tank force. A tank program was studied by the Research and Armament Inspectorate in 1920, but its July 1920 report proposed a bewildering variety of specialized tank types at a time when there was simply no money. The chief of the general staff, Gén Edmond Buat, rejected the findings and recommended that the future tank program be confined to the development of an improved infantry tank and a breakthrough tank (*char de rupture*). There was a proliferation of experimental designs and paper design studies in the 1920s, but very little new manufacture until the mid-1930s.

THE OTHER LEGACY TANK: CHAR DE RUPTURE 2C

The most impressive tank to have emerged from World War I was the Char de Rupture 2C. This massive land-battleship had been assigned to the FCM ship-builders and constructed in the Chantiers Navals de la Seyne dockyard. The firm had completed a pilot FCM 1A heavy tank prior to the end of the war, and on February 21, 1918 was given a contract to build 300 improved Char 2C by March 1919 for a final offensive against Germany. With the war's end, the contract was trimmed back to ten tanks. The complexity of the design caused manufacturing delays, and the tanks were not delivered until 1921.

The Char 2C was remarkable for its size and complexity. It weighed 70 metric tons, and used hybrid propulsion consisting of two conventional engines that powered electric generators which in turn supplied electricity to a pair of electric traction motors. The original plan was to use a pair of 100hp engines, but these were not adequate. Once the war ended, FCM had access to German Zeppelin engines, which had been acquired as war reparations, and used 250hp Maybach engines. The tank was armed with a 75mm M1897 gun in the main turret, two sponson machine guns, and a separate machine-gun turret in the rear. In 1923, one of the tanks was converted into the Char 2C Bis, armed with a short 155mm howitzer instead of the usual 75mm gun.

The tank was so massive that normal transport means were out of the question. Instead, the Char 2C was moved long distances by means of a special railroad system. The tank itself was attached to a pair of special transport bogies. Each company of three tanks traveled in a special railroad convoy consisting of two locomotives and 30 other railcars for the crews, supplies, and supporting vehicles.

The Char 2C remained in service through 1940 and was mobilized with the 511e RCC in June 1940. Two of the tanks broke down with mechanical problems, so two company trains with the six remaining tanks departed their base northwest of Metz on June 12. After surviving an air attack on June 14, the two trains became trapped on June 15 between advancing German units and a section of damaged track northeast of Langres. To prevent their capture, Commandant Fournet decided to sabotage the tanks using explosive charges. As a result, these old dinosaurs never saw combat.

The six remaining Char 2C tanks were lost when their special transport trains were trapped northeast of Langres; they were sabotaged by their crews on the evening of June 15, 1940. This image provides a good view of the rear machine turret on the Char 2C, as well as details of the special rail carriage. (NARA)

No doubt the most impressive tank to have emerged from World War I was the FCM Char 2C breakthrough tank. This was a popular subject for press coverage in the 1930s, and this shows tank 97 "Normandie" on public display. (NARA)

MODERNIZING THE FT

One of the main drawbacks of the Renault FT was its slow speed and jarring cross-country ride. As a result, there were several schemes to improve the suspension. The first effort involved the use of a new Kégresse suspension with a metal/rubber band track. A pilot was completed in late 1922 and 23 were converted in 1924. About half of these were deployed to Morocco during the Rif War in 1925. In 1928, a further six were converted using an improved track. One of the main problems undercutting Renault FT modernization was the lack of funds. From 1920 to 1929, French spending on tanks totaled only FF4.1 million (~$160,000).

Work on further suspension improvements continued in 1924 as the Renault NC 1. The intention of this program was to develop a tank capable of road travel comparable to an automobile, while not sacrificing cross-country performance. Unlike the Kégresse option, the baseline NC 1 used metal track. An alternative was built with Kégresse suspension as the NC 2. Aside from the three pilots, 25 tanks were manufactured, one each

BOTTOM LEFT
The first attempt to modernize the Renault FT, starting in 1924, substituted the Kégresse suspension to provide better road speed. (NARA)

BOTTOM RIGHT
A second batch of ten modernized Renault-Kégresse tanks was sold to Yugoslavia in 1930 and saw combat with the 1.bataljona bornih kola during the fighting with the Wehrmacht in Macedonia in 1941. This rear view shows the drums that replaced the earlier tail-skid as a trench-crossing aid. (NARA)

The Renault NC substituted a vertical spring suspension. A total of 23 NC 2s were exported to Japan and they were used by Captain Shigemi's 2nd Independent Tank Company during the fighting in Shanghai in 1932. (NARA)

going to Poland and Sweden, and 23 being sold to Japan. A final attempt to develop a dedicated export tank, the NC 3, was undertaken in 1928.

In spite of the improvement offered by the suspension alterations, there was little urgency to upgrade the vast tank fleet of Renault FT through the early 1930s. The one area where modernization was approved was in the tank armament. The Char FT Mitrailleuse (machine gun) had been armed with the Hotchkiss 8mm machine gun, and there was some interest in replacing this weapon with the Reibel 7.5mm MAC, which used a more practical drum magazine instead of the clip used with the Hotchkiss. Although this was approved in 1929, a contract was not awarded until 1933. This required a new mantlet and a new internal ammunition stowage system, which was finalized in 1934. In total, some 1,000 Renault FT tanks were approved for conversion. These were sometimes called FT Mle. 1931 or FT 17/31.

CHAR LÉGER D1

The first effort substantially to improve the basic Renault FT began in 1927, due to the recognition that Renault NC only addressed the suspension and not other characteristics such as armor or firepower. A new "NC modifié" light tank was developed in 1928 with thicker 30mm armor, a more powerful 47mm gun with coaxial machine gun, and a more powerful Renault 25CV (74hp) engine, which permitted a higher road speed of 18km/h (11mph). The new design resembled the FT in general layout, but was significantly larger and heavier. The hull accommodated a third crewman to operate the new radio. Trials continued through 1929 and the new design was accepted for service in October 1929 as the Char Léger D1. The decision to proceed

When the Char D1 was first delivered in 1931, the turret was not yet ready. As a result, it was temporarily fitted with Renault FT turrets, as seen here during the summer 1931 army maneuvers. (NARA)

with manufacture required a major expansion of French army tank funding. It increased more than twentyfold from the previous decade to FF81.5 million (~$3.2 million) between 1930 and 1934. Production began in 1931, with the first tank delivered in October that year and the final example of the 160 tanks in May 1935. Production problems with the new cast turret led to the temporary adoption of Renault FT Char Canon 37mm gun turrets. The first batch of ten Schneider ST1 turrets proved to be poorly balanced, requiring the addition of rear turret counterweights. This original batch remained in service as training tanks. The definitive Schneider ST2 turret was adopted on the rest of the tanks. Since these were the only modern French tanks available in the early 1930s, the three D1 battalions saw extensive usage. By 1937, many of the D1 tanks were already worn out, and they were rather old-fashioned compared to new types that were appearing. As a result, they were sent to Tunisia in 1937 except for some school tanks. Of these units, the 67e BCC returned to France in 1940, where it took part in the June campaign.

The definitive version of the Char D1 used the new ST2 turret. This is an example in service in Tunisia in 1943. (NARA)

THE ARMS RACE OF THE LATE 1930s

As of January 1, 1937, the three D1 tank battalions were the only ones in French army service equipped with modern tanks, and these were largely worn out from extensive use. Ominous developments in Germany made it clear that a major rearmament program would be necessary. The Nazi rise to power in Germany in 1933, the renunciation of the Versailles treaty limits on German armaments in May 1935, and the remilitarization of the Rhineland in March 1936 were all hints that a new German threat was on the rise. This began an arms race that played a critical role in the 1940 Battle of France.

With regard to infantry tanks, in 1933 the army decided to replace the entire Renault FT inventory with a new design. In 1934, Gén Maurice Gamelin set the goal as 16 battalions (800 tanks) by January 1938 and 46 battalions (2,500 tanks) by 1940. In terms of the *char puissant*, the plans aimed to provide 500 B1 and D2 tanks. This required a very substantial industrial investment since it was based on a goal of manufacturing about 80 infantry tanks per month. Until 1936, there was hardly any tank industry in France. The Renault automotive firm based at Billancourt near Paris had retained a small cadre of engineers for tank development underwritten by corporate funding. Renault maintained the small AMX tank assembly workshop nearby in Issy-les-Moulineaux. Production methods were artisanal and depended on a scattered network of subcontractors to provide parts. Between 1931 and 1935, French industry had only been producing about three tanks per month.

In May 1936, the Popular Front came to power in France, a coalition of center and leftwing political parties. The Popular Front supported a French rearmament program, but at the same time its domestic policies created an enormous amount of turmoil within the French industry that hindered a timely implementation of such a program. Due to public clamor over alleged "war-profiteering," the new government decided to nationalize several of the commercial firms involved in tank development and production, including Renault's tank research bureau, the Hotchkiss armaments research

The 67e BCC returned to France from Tunisia in 1940 and took part in the summer campaign. This D1 tank was lost in the fighting near Suippes in June 1940. This photo accentuates the large frame on the right side used to mount the antenna for the tank's ER51/ER52 radio sets. (NARA)

The initial production series of the Char D2 was fitted with the APX-1 turret with the short 47 SA34 gun, as seen in this corporate publicity photo of tank no. 2006 "Rocroi" in 1937 with the early camouflage scheme. (Patton Museum)

bureau, Schneider's armor plate plant (ACT/Atelier des Locomotives) at Le Creusot, and the Renault AMX tank assembly workshop.

Labor reforms introduced by the government further increased the disruption. The adoption of a 40-hour working week and accompanying labor unrest often meant that armament plants were limited to a 40-hour week, since the trade unions were unwilling to permit multiple shifts. This led to delays in the completion of tank orders. For example, of the 1,315 new infantry tanks that were contracted for delivery by August 1938, only 767 (58 percent) were delivered on time. Another impact of the labor reforms was a steady escalation in labor costs and a resultant inflation in tank prices. Combined with the decline in the value of the franc after the government dropped the gold standard in 1936, tank prices skyrocketed. For example, the first batches of Renault R35 tanks ordered in 1936 cost about FF180,000, but this climbed steadily to FF285,000 in 1938 and to FF355,000 by 1940. Renault was trapped in a "cost scissors" between the prices fixed in the original contracts and rising labor and material costs. These issues were not resolved until after 1937 and added further delays.

While political interference and labor unrest were partly responsible for the problems in army modernization, the French army itself was another source of delay. Army procurement policy was a leftover from the threadbare days of the 1920s and led to adversarial relations with the industry. The army usually issued tank production contracts in small batches rather than as a multi-year program. This was done to impose quality control over tank deliveries, with the result that the subsequent contract was not issued until the previous contracts were satisfactorily fulfilled. In practice, these policies created more bureaucratic impediments to time-critical modernization efforts. The outcome of these various impediments was to slow the delivery of tanks to the French army, which in turn delayed the timely formation and training of new tank units. This would significantly undermine the tank force in 1940, since so many tanks were not delivered until a few months before the German attack. While France produced more tanks than Germany by May 1940, it lost the arms race since the deliveries were too late. Most French tank units were formed so late that they were poorly trained and inexperienced with their new tanks.

INFANTRY TANK ORGANIZATION IN 1940

The French army was an enthusiastic proponent of tanks, but its mechanization effort was split between the infantry and cavalry. Tanks played a vital role in the 1918 French victory, and so remained a central element of infantry doctrine. The inspector general of the infantry in 1938 remarked that

> my profound conviction is that these machines are destined to play a decisive role in a future conflict; the infantry was unable to do without tanks in the last war and will be able even less in future operations. The tank must be the preferred arm in a nation poor in personnel. War is a question of force where the advantage rests with the most powerful machine and not with the most rapid machine.

France's development of an armored force was shaped by its profoundly defensive strategic outlook in the 1930s. Infantry tanks were primarily intended to accompany the infantry into battle, much as in 1918, and not to serve as an offensive strike force comparable to German panzer divisions. The bulk of the French army's tank force in May 1940 was located in the separate battalions of accompanying tanks, numbering 1,540 tanks in May 1940, or about half the tank force. Under the new French tactical doctrine formulated with the creation of the new armored divisions in 1939, two basic roles for infantry tanks were recognized, the *char d'accompagnement* (accompanying tank) and the *char de manoeuvre* (maneuver tank). The accompanying tanks were deployed in tank battalions subordinated to infantry corps and divisions, while the maneuver tanks were deployed with the armored divisions.

The basic infantry tank organization was the tank battalion (BCC: *bataillon de chars de combat*). By 1940, there were 41 tank battalions in metropolitan France and eight more in the colonies in North Africa and the Levant. These had a nominal strength of 45 tanks, each consisting of three companies (13 each), and a reserve company (six). Each tank company was organized into four tank platoons with four tanks each and one tank with the command

A rear view of a Char D2 from the second production batch (2083) of the 350e CACC at Périgueux, which can be distinguished by the use of the later PPLRX-180P episcope on the turret. Although not apparent from this angle, this tank was armed with the later 47 SA35 gun. There were plans to retrofit the D2 with a trench-crossing tail, but manufacture was not ready by the summer of 1940. (Patton Museum)

The original Renault ZM pilot was equipped with a cast turret armed with two machine guns. This configuration was short-lived and the pilot was refitted with a gun-armed turret. (Patton Museum)

sections. The exceptions to this organization were the battalions still equipped with the obsolete Renault FT tank, which had 63 tanks per battalion.

The basic mission of the accompanying tank battalions was direct infantry support. The tank battalions were distributed to the field armies, which in turn assigned them to the corps to carry out their mission. As often as not, the corps distributed the battalions to individual infantry divisions. The French army considered the tank company to be the basic tactical unit of the tank force, meaning that tank units were not supposed to be deployed on a scale smaller than a company. In the early summer of 1940, the army formed a number of autonomous companies (CACC: *compagnie autonome de chars de combat*) to employ tanks delivered too late to form into battalions.

UNIT ORGANIZATION: THE FRENCH DCR

The infantry's interest in armored divisions was belated and grudging. This was in part due to decisions earlier in the 1930s to favor the cavalry as the mobile arm of decision. The French cavalry recognized the failure of horse cavalry in World War I and enthusiastically embraced mechanization to maintain its rationale as the army's mobile force. Gén Maxime Weygand, the chief of the general staff in the mid-1930s, had favored the mechanization of the cavalry as a means to build up an offensive armored strike force. The cavalry began the process of forming mechanized divisions (DLM: *division légère mécanique*) before the infantry's armored divisions. The 1e DLM formed in 1935–36, and by the time of the 1940 campaign, three of these divisions were in service. In May 1940, about 835 or roughly a quarter of the army's tanks were in cavalry units.

Gén Estienne had fostered the *chars puissants* such as the Char B and Char D to serve in a mobile role in the vanguard of infantry corps or for other maneuver missions. His views fell out of favor in the early 1930s. Young firebrands like Col Charles de Gaulle advocated the creation of offensively oriented armored divisions. His views were deemed too radical, not due to their tactical content but owing to his insistence that they could only be effective if manned by a professional cadre. This viewpoint ran counter to French politics in the 1930s, which was still profoundly antiwar after the savage losses of 1914–18, as well as to the Republican tradition of the *levée en masse* over professional armies.

Even as late as 1936, army chief-of-staff Gén Gamelin noted that "the problems of constituting large tank units has been studied in France since 1932; the development of the antitank weapon has caused a renunciation of this concept." The German formation of panzer divisions and the extensive use of tanks during the Spanish Civil War between 1936 and 1938 kept this

The Renault ZM pilot was modified to accommodate the new APX-R turret, seen here in its pre-series configuration. The numerous rectangular shapes bolted to the hull are test weights to simulate the actual weight of a production tank. (Patton Museum)

controversy broiling.[2] In 1938, the Superior War Council ordered the infantry's tank inspector to study a large armored unit consisting of two Char B1 battalions, a battalion of D2, two motorized infantry battalions and two motorized artillery battalions. A provisional manual on the tactical employment of armored divisions was released for comment in February 1939. The tactical doctrine still did not envision the armored division as an autonomous force, but rather as part of an infantry corps to assist in the maneuver of infantry divisions. The German demonstration of the combat potential of panzer divisions in Poland in 1939 ended the French dithering about armored divisions.

The formation of three armored divisions (DCr: *division cuirassée*) did not begin until January–March 1940. The core of the new armored divisions was a pair of tank demibrigades with two battalions of Char B1 bis and two battalions of Hotchkiss H39. The DCr was smaller and less powerful than a German panzer division and was not a balanced combined-arms force. The DCr was only half the strength of a panzer division, about 6,155 men

The initial production batches of the R35 used the early version of the APX-R turret that was fitted with the original Fente Estienne binocular view ports, as seen on this tank on exercise in 1937. (NARA)

versus over 13,000 men, due to its extremely small infantry component and its lack of a reconnaissance element. Likewise, the tank strength of the DCr was only about 160 tanks versus an average of 265 tanks in the panzer divisions in May 1940. In addition to their weak organization, the delay in organizing these divisions significantly reduced their battlefield effectiveness, since they had little if any combined training before the start of the Battle of France. The six Char B1 bis battalions in the first three DCr were not fully equipped until the spring of 1940, and their crews were in most cases only partially trained.

---

2   Steven Zaloga, *Spanish Civil War Tanks: The Proving Ground for Blitzkrieg*, Osprey New Vanguard 170, 2010.

In contrast, the German army had begun the formation of its panzer divisions five years earlier along with the cavalry's light mechanized divisions (*leichte division*) shortly after. By 1938, five panzer divisions and four light divisions had been organized. After the army's combat experiences in Poland in 1939, the light divisions were quickly converted to panzer divisions. The French army never had the opportunity to rationalize its light mechanized divisions and armored divisions.

An overhead view of the Renault R35 preserved for many years at the Ordnance Museum at Aberdeen Proving Ground. The camouflage scheme is attractive but inaccurate, and the markings are a hodge-podge of French and Italian insignia. This particular tank was captured from the Italian 101° Battaglione carri on Sicily during Operation *Husky* in July 1943. (Author)

CHAR PUISSANT D2

With production of the Char Léger D1 underway, Renault proposed its Renault UZ Char de Combat Surblindé (uparmored tank) as a further evolution of the D1. This design increased the armor from 30 to 40mm, and employed the larger Renault 40CV (150hp) engine. One of the underlying reasons for the design was anxiety over a possible weight limit on future tanks being considered by the French government as part of the international disarmament conference being held in Geneva at the time. By this stage, Renault was deeply involved in the development of the new Char B battle tank, but this design would exceed the proposed weight limits.

B

RENAULT R35, 3e COMPANIE, 21e BCC, ALSACE, JUNE 1940

This is the tank of Capitaine Pierre Perat, who commanded the 3e Companie, 21e BCC during the battalion's fighting in the Alsace in June 1940. This battalion had extremely elaborate markings, with the companies carrying a large letter on the turret side: H (1e Co.), S (2e Co.), and V (3e Co.). In Perat's 3e Companie, the "V" on the left side of the turret was followed by the section number, for example V2 for a tank of the 2e Section. In Perat's case, he used his own initial, so it read VP. On the right side of the turret, the company letter was not carried, but instead a name was painted on the front side of the turret followed by the section number. In Perat's case, this was "L'Aiglon" (Little Eagle) followed by "P." Perat's tank also carried a distinctive rank insignia on the two rear turret corners. Besides these unit insignia, the tanks typically carried the national cocarde (roundel) on the front and rear, which had been ordered in June 1940 to reduce instances of fratricide. The white circles on the front and rear were night-driving aids, another campaign addition most often seen in the final weeks of the fighting. The "flaming grenade" on the hull pannier is a standard French army weight class marking. This particular tank is painted in one of the more elaborate Renault schemes, seen mainly on tanks from the 1937–38 contract batches delivered from May 1937 to June 1939. The unusually vivid camouflage scheme stemmed from an artillery branch camouflage program of March 10, 1937 that established 15 camouflage colors in three families: sky shades, earth shades and shadow shades. The Renault practice was to use the sky colors on the upper portions of the tank, the earth colors in bands along the center, and the shadow shades below. There were complaints that the new tanks had eight colors, four of them rather vivid, which defeated the purpose of camouflage. As a result, the manufacturers were ordered to go back to the more modest style recommended in 1938 instructions.

The standard production version of the Renault R35 had the improved APX-R1 turret with the PPLRX-180P episcope, as seen on this preserved example that was displayed at the June 2012 Eurosatory exhibition outside Paris. (Author)

Three UZ pilots were built and they underwent trials between 1932 and 1934. They were armed with the same 47 SA34 semiautomatic tank gun as the D1, but in a substantially improved APX-1 turret. The general staff had very mixed feelings about the need for such tanks, and in August 1933 Renault was officially informed that the program would be dropped in favor of a new effort for a small and less expensive infantry tank. Since credits had already been approved for the Char D2, an initial production contract was awarded to Renault on December 29, 1934 for 50 tanks. The deliveries from Renault took place from January to November 1935, but problems with turret casting at the Usine de Batignoles delayed the delivery of completed tanks until April 1936–February 1937. Due to the general shortage of tanks, a second contract for 50 more D2 tanks was approved in May 1937, and awarded to Renault and AMX in June 1938. About 37 were delivered in the weeks preceding the start of the 1940 campaign. The second production batch was built with an improved turret fitted with the new 47mm SA35 tank gun as used on the Char B1 bis. Many of the tanks from the first batch were rearmed with the long 47 SA35 gun prior to the 1940 campaign. The Char D2 fell between the usual size range of the *char léger* infantry tanks and larger Char B battle tanks. It might have remained a rare curiosity were it not for the fact that it served in combat in 1940 in the partially formed 4e DCr commanded by a little-known officer, Charles de Gaulle.

CHAR LÉGER MLE. 1935 R (RENAULT R35)

The most numerous and important French infantry tank of the 1940 campaign was the Renault R35. The substantial increase in size and weight of the Renault D1 and the later D2 steered them away from the traditional infantry support role of the Renault FT and towards the battle tank mission that was already being addressed by the Char B. With the widespread recognition that the Renault FT was obsolete, the general staff in 1933 decided against pursuing the D2 program in favor of the production of a new small infantry tank. Since the French army had shifted to a program of one-year conscription in 1930, a major concern in the infantry tank requirements was the development of a very simple tank that could be easily operated and maintained by non-professional tank troops. The basic requirement called for a 6-ton tank "with small dimensions, reliable, inexpensive and easily maintained."

The Hotchkiss firm had already caught wind of the requirement, and convinced the Armament Advisory Council (Conseil Consultatif de l'Armement) of the merits of a turretless accompanying tank, which was displayed to the committee in mock-up form. A contract for three pilot tanks was awarded to Hotchkiss on June 30, 1933 even before the formal infantry tank specifications had been issued.

The specifications were released to industry on August 2, 1933 and led to offers from 14 companies and government agencies. The government APX workshop was funded to provide a pilot tank, and it was eventually assigned to design the cast turret for the winning model. Four commercial firms were awarded contracts to build prototypes, Renault, FCM, Delaunay-Belleville, and Batignolles-Châtillon. Of these, pilot models were built by all except Delaunay-Belleville.

Renault completed its ZM design before Hotchkiss in spite of the latter's head start. The first two Hotchkiss pilots did not appear until January 1935, and by the time the pilots appeared, the specification had been superseded to incorporate thicker armor. In the event, the Hotchkiss design was rejected. Although significantly cheaper than the Renault design, it suffered from a weak powerplant, poor internal volume and poor vision devices. Hotchkiss hurriedly redesigned the third pilot, incorporating the new APX-R turret as used on the Renault design. However, by this stage, the Renault design had been accepted.

The Renault ZM pilot used a cast hull and cast turret armed with two machine guns. The extensive use of armor castings was a significant innovation that was expected to lower the production cost of the tank, and the casting effort was a joint program between Renault and several industrial firms including Schneider, Imphy, and Ugine. Early trials revealed numerous technical problems with the design, not the least of which was the excessive weight of the pilot tank. With the German army's decision to adopt a 37mm antitank gun, Gén P. M. Velpry, Inspecteur Général des Chars, insisted that armor be increased from 30mm to 40mm. As a result, the specifications were modified in May 1934, raising the weight limit to 8 tons. The Renault ZM pilot was sent back to the plant for heavy reconstruction, and in April 1934 the first of the new APX-R turrets arrived. This was designed by the government APX bureau and cast at the Atelier de Rueil, hence its designation. It was used on both the second Renault ZM pilot and on the third Hotchkiss pilot. The armament consisted of the same 37mm SA18 gun as the FT tank. It was also fitted with a coaxial 7.5mm machine gun. Propulsion was an 85hp Renault 447 engine, a commercial type used in Renault trucks and buses.

The tests uncovered a number of problems with the Renault suspension, but in view of the deteriorating international situation, the French army

ABOVE LEFT
The APX-R turret was designed for a single crewman and was accessed through a rear hatch. This interior view shows the breech of the 37 SA18 gun. The telescopic sight on the left and the coaxial machine gun on the right are missing in this view. (NARA)

ABOVE RIGHT
The predominant French tank weapon in 1940 was the same 37 SA18 gun used on the Renault FT. However, it was mounted in a new cast mantlet and was accompanied by a coaxial 7.5mm machine gun. This is one of the later APX-R turrets with the PPLRX-180P episcope. (Author)

Lingering problems with the R35 suspension led to the substitution of an AMX design using vertical coil springs. This company illustration shows the configuration of the new R40 suspension. (Patton Museum)

decided to proceed to production with the Renault ZM. An initial contract for the first batch of 300 was awarded to Renault in April 1935. The new tank was designated as Char Léger mle. 1935 R, though it was often known as the Renault R35. The first production tank was delivered on March 24, 1936. The production of the R35 involved many factories, since at the time the French industry no longer had a plant capable of tank manufacture. The Renault plant at Billancourt outside Paris manufactured most of the mechanical sub-components of the tank, the turret castings were undertaken at foundries in Cail and Fives-Lille, the hull castings were produced at the St Chamond and Alsthom foundries, the plate armor was produced at Creusot, the hull assembled at the Alsthom factory in Tarbes, the weapons and optics came from Puteaux, and the final assembly took place at the AMX plant at Issy-les-Moulineaux outside Paris. The first two tank battalions were mobilized on June 1, 1937 for the new tank, 9e BCC and 20e BCC. In total, some 1,611 tanks were ordered including export tanks and the improved R40, of which about 1,570 were delivered prior to the fall of France in June 1940.

In the summer of 1937, some R35s were subjected to firing trials at Bourges using the 25mm antitank gun, and it was found that the cast armor had some significant irregularities in protective quality. This led to improvements in the armor in the subsequent production batches. The original APX-R turrets used a binocular Fente Estienne diascope for

C FCM 36, 1e COMPANIE, 7e BCC, SEDAN, MAY 1940

The FCM 36 was generally painted by FCM in a distinctive pattern with light grey blue (*gris bleu clair*) or pale yellow (*jaunâtre*) at the top, and horizontal rolling bands of red brown (*sépia*), pale green (*réséda*), beige, and dark green (*vert foncé*). The 7e BCC usually used a distinctive circular emblem on the turret front, based on the regimental insignia of the 503e RCC, a stylized tanker firing a machine gun. It was reproduced in company colors with the 1e Companie in all blue, the 2e Companie with the gear in white, and the 3e Companie with the gear in red. This is the tank of the commander of the 4e Section, 1e Companie, Aspirant (réserve) Pierre Cassier, named "Le Téméraire" (Reckless). Although not visible from this angle, the turret had a medium blue "club" insignia on both turret rear corners, about 30cm (1 foot) high. This followed the French tank tradition since World War I of using playing card symbols to distinguish subunits. The order in this unit was 1e Section (spade), 2e Section (heart), 3e Section (Diamond) and 4e Section (Club). These were in the company color (1e Companie: blue, 2e Companie: white, 3e Companie: red).

The production version of the R40 tank incorporated the late features for this series, including the long 37 SA38 gun and the unditching tail. This is an example lost in the June 1940 fighting. (NARA)

the three vision devices on the turret sides that proved vulnerable to projectile impacts. It was replaced in 1938 on the modernized APX-R1 turret with the PPLRX-180P episcope, which can be distinguished by its more streamlined shape and simple view slit.

The specifications of the R35 had retained the old 37mm gun on the assumption that the principal role for the tank was fighting non-armored targets such as enemy troops and earthwork defenses. The French army had experienced no tank-vs-tank fighting during World War I, so the armor penetration features of the gun were not a high priority. The first large-scale use of tanks since World War I took place during the Spanish Civil War, and instances of tank-vs-tank fighting were commonplace. This led to the development of the longer 37 SA38 gun, which offered better antiarmor penetration (30mm vs 15mm at 1,000m). This gun was introduced on the later production batches of the R35 after gun production began in the second half of 1939.

Although the French army had pioneered the use of radios on tanks with the Char FT TSF during World War I, the original requirement for the R35 did not include a radio. The presumption was that it would add too much cost and complexity to the tank, and take up too much internal volume. Experimentation with the new ER54 radio based on the ER40 infantry radio began at Camp de Sissonne in April 1937. Prior to the outbreak of the war in 1939, no radio-equipped R35 tanks were in service except for the 45 R35 tanks deployed with the 2e Bataillon, 507e RCC, which was assigned to study the issue of radio use in infantry tanks. A program to deploy radios in section and company command tanks took place in the spring of 1940.

The susceptibility of the R35 to bogging in soft soil led to a variety of efforts to improve its cross-country capability. Several different suspension options were studied between 1938 and 1939, with the army finally deciding on February 16, 1939 on the AMX system, which used vertical springs and plate track. AMX also developed a tail to improve the tank's trench-crossing capability. The tails began to be added to R35 tanks in late 1939 around tank No. 1100. The plan was to switch production to the Char Léger mle. 1935 R modifié 1939 (Renault R40) at tank number 1500. Delays in manufacturing the components delayed this switch, and about 155 were completed.

Aside from the Renault FT, the Renault R35 was the only French tank exported in significant numbers until 1940. The first batch of 50 R35 tanks was delivered to Poland in the late summer of 1939 for the 21 Batalion Czołgów Lekkich. A second battalion was on order, but Poland's defeat in 1939 led to its diversion to French units in the Levant. Partially formed Polish R35 companies saw some combat against both German and Soviet forces during the September 1939 campaign. The Red Army captured a few examples and the preserved R35 tank at the Kubinka museum is one of these Polish tanks. Most of the Polish tanks were in southeastern Galicia, so 34 escaped into neighboring Romania and a few to Hungary. Romania had planned to begin licensed production of the R35, and 200 were ordered. A total of 41 was delivered in 1940 before the Battle of France ended production. France delivered 54 R35s to Yugoslavia in April 1940 and they saw combat use in the short 1941 campaign there. France delivered a single battalion of 50 R35 tanks to Turkey in January 1940.

The FCM 36 was strikingly different from the Renault and Hotchkiss infantry tanks due to the use of welded construction and its unique multifaceted hull. Although widely regarded as the best infantry tank of its generation, it was too expensive and so was produced in modest numbers. This is an example from the 4e BCC, with its mantlet painted in the national *tricolore*. (NARA)

CHAR LÉGER FCM 36

Although the R35 was selected as the principal infantry tank in the 1934 competition, the FCM entry was promising enough that the French army decided to place a contract for 100 tanks on June 5, 1936. In contrast to the Renault and Hotchkiss entries, the FCM 36 employed advanced welded construction, which was not entirely surprising since its manufacturer was primarily involved in building warships. Another difference was the decision to use a diesel engine. This tank was originally powered by a Berliet 95hp ACRO diesel, but problems with this engine led to the

The FCM 36 of the 503e RCC paraded down the Champs-Elysées in Paris on two occasions: the November 11, 1938 Joan of Arc day parade and the July 14, 1939 national holiday. During the 1940 campaign, this tank served in the 7e BCC and was lost during the Sedan fighting on the road from Maisonette to Chémery on May 14, 1940. (NARA)

The turret interior of the FCM 36 was more spacious than APX-R used on the other infantry tanks, and there were plans to mount it on the Renault R35. (Author)

substitution of the Berliet 91hp Ricardo diesel. The FCM 36 turret was considered to be so superior to the APX-R turret that plans were underway to substitute this turret on the R35, starting with tank 1,350. However, the turret proved to be less adaptable to the new 37 SA38 gun, so this scheme proved stillborn. The use of a rear-mounted transmission provided more space in the fighting compartment, and so radio use on this type was more common than on the R35. The ER54 radio was the type most often used, but in 1940 some received the ER28 set.

E

1: HOTCHKISS H39, 2/26e BCC, 1e DCR, MAY 1940

The tanks of the 26e BCC used the usual playing card symbols, but in a square with rounded corners. This was carried on either side of the turret and on the upper right corner of the rear. The 2e Compagnie used a large letter on the hull side to identify section commanders, in this case the 4e Section, "U" (registration number 40580). Other examples include R (spade insignia, no. 40582), S (heart insignia, no. 40501), and T (diamond insignia, no. 40530). The unit commanders generally had tanks with the 37 SA38, and in view of the production date of these vehicles, this gun must have been retrofitted. The French tank specialist Pascal Danjou has made an extensive study of French tank camouflage, and he has identified six sequential Hotchkiss camouflage schemes during the H35–H39 production run. This fourth type, consisting of a pale green over the usual French army dark green, started around no. 40569 and continued through 40900. A few of the battalion's tanks, such as this one, had the battalion insignia painted on them, a boar's head on a shield with the phrase "Je grogne" ("I growl").

2: HOTCHKISS H38, COMPANIE AUTONOME, 42e BCC (1/42e BCC), JUNE 1940

In the wake of the gaudy camouflage schemes of 1936–37, the engineers conducted tests, which concluded that the elaborate color schemes were counterproductive. In August 1938, a new set of instructions was issued recommending a simple two-color scheme of grey-green (*gris vert*) and dark earth (*terre d'ombre*) that became the common style on late production tanks in 1939 and 1940. This tank (no. 40979) has this late camouflage scheme, the sixth type used on the Hotchkiss, which appeared beginning around tank no. 40957. The 42e BCC had its 1e Compagnie broken off in the spring of 1940 to create the 342e Compagnie autonome that was sent to Norway with the Allied expeditionary force. In its place, it was supposed to receive a company from the 48e BCC. However, this company did not arrive in time, and it fought on its own during the campaign, sometimes referred to as 1/42e BCC. As seen in this example, its markings were very simple.

1

2

The FCM 36 was widely regarded as the best of the new infantry tanks, but the advanced welding techniques resulted in production delays and the two battalions were not delivered until May 1938 to March 1939. The main reason that more FCM 36s were not ordered was the higher priority afforded to the construction of the Char B1 bis at FCM, the limited production capacity at the plant, and the high cost. The first batch cost FF450,000 while at the same time the R35 cost only about FF200,000. Two more contracts were planned in 1940 totaling a further 300 tanks, but these contracts were never awarded due to the estimated price tag of FF900,000 compared to a contemporary cost of around FF350,000 for the late-model Renault R35.

The infantry received two battalions of the H35, which served with the 13e and 38e BCC in 1940, with registration numbers in the 40301–40400 block. The H35 can be distinguished from the later and more common H39 by the smaller rear engine casting and the forward pointing muffler. (NARA)

CAVALRY TANK FOR THE INFANTRY: THE HOTCHKISS H35 AND H39

During the competition for the new infantry tank between 1933 and 1934, Hotchkiss prepared a third pilot that was fitted with the same APX-R turret as the R35. The infantry had already selected the Renault R35, and so the Hotchkiss seemed destined for limbo. Under somewhat murky circumstances, the minister of war, Jean Fabry, saw a demonstration of the Hotchkiss at Vincennes and decided it was a better choice than the new Somua. In spite

The two first pilot designs of the Hotchkiss infantry tank offering used a fixed casemate armed with up to two 7.5mm machine guns. This configuration was quickly rejected and the third pilot was fitted with an APX-R turret. (Patton Museum)

of army opposition, Hotchkiss was awarded a contract on November 6, 1935 for 200 H35 tanks for the cavalry. These were delivered from July 1936 through July 1937, though without their turrets. A second contract followed on September 7, 1936 for 100 more. During deliberations over the 1937–40 armament program, the requirement for infantry tanks was increased to 2,500 tanks, which was beyond the capacity of Renault and FCM for the foreseeable future. Gamelin decided to authorize additional Hotchkiss production, this time for the infantry. This was strongly opposed by Gén Julien Dufieux, the infantry's inspector general for tanks. Nonetheless, Hotchkiss was awarded a contract on January 23, 1937 for 100 tanks for the infantry, with delivery taking place between July and September 1938. These were eventually issued to the 13e BCC and 38e BCC.

The Hotchkiss H35 was not popular in either cavalry or infantry service. The cavalry in particular was very critical of its slow speed and its mechanical faults, such as the tendency of its road-wheels to shed their rubber tire. Hotchkiss began a redesign effort, first trying to replace the original 60hp engine with a new 117hp type that had been designed for Hotchkiss Monte Carlo race-cars. Initial trials with this engine were unsuccessful since the new engine proved too powerful for the transmission and gear box. After more improvements, a 120hp variant was finally selected. This also caused the redesign of the rear hull casting to accommodate the larger powerplant. Hotchkiss also modified the suspension, adopting new metal-rimmed road-wheels and shifting from the original 25cm track to a new 27cm track (9.8–10.6in). Hotchkiss referred to the new version as "Char Léger mle. 1938 series D," sometimes abbreviated as 38H. This designation was not adopted

Specifications

Crew	4
Length	6.37m (20.8ft)
Width	2.5m (8.2ft)
Height	2.79m (9.2ft)
Combat weight	31.5 metric tonnes (34.6 tons)
Hull gun	75mm SA 35 L/17, 74 rounds
Turret gun	47mm SA 35 L/32, 50 rounds
Machine guns	2 7.5mm Riebel MAC 31, 5,100 rounds
Engine	Renault 307 hp V-6
Fuel	400 liters (105 gallons)
Range	180km (112m)
Top speed	27km/h (17mph)
Armor	60mm front, 60mm side, 55mm rear

KEY

1. Muffler
2. Engine transmission
3. Naeder steering system
4. Engine radiator
5. Renault engine
6. Insulated Radio antenna
7. Guard to prevent 47mm gun from striking rear of tank
8. 47mm ammunition stowage
9. Turret traverse
10. Commander's vision cupola
11. Driver's station
12. 47mm SA 35 gun
13. Driver's controls
14. 75mm SA 35 gun
15. Mud chute
16. 75mm gun breech
17. Side access door
18. Engine firewall/bulkhead
19. Attachment for jack extension for track repair
20. Drive sprocket

The final production batches of the Hotchkiss H39 in May–June 1940 were armed with the 37mm SA38 gun and were fitted with an unditching tail. This is a batch of tanks in the Hotchkiss factory lot in Saint-Denis prior to their dispatch to units. (APGOM)

by the army, which called it the "Char Léger mle. 1935 H modifié 1939" or H39. The slow pace of Somua cavalry tank deliveries led to further cavalry contracts for the H39 in July 1938, eventually totaling 400.

The infantry acquisition of the Hotchkiss would have ended after the first batch of H35s were it not for the deteriorating international situation. As of February 1, 1939, only 1,310 light tanks of the 2,800 on order had been delivered. Once again, Gamelin pressured the infantry into accepting more of the Hotchkiss, in this case the improved H39. More than half of the 1938 contract batch was assigned to infantry tank battalions, along with another batch of 80 ordered in April 1939. Most of the infantry H39s went to tank battalions assigned to the armored divisions rather than battalions assigned to infantry support.

As was the case with the R35, the army wanted firepower and mobility improvements on their H39 tanks. The new 37mm SA38 gun began to be delivered in 1940, with an initial aim to fit one out of four infantry tanks with the gun until there were enough to equip all new production tanks. As of the end of April 1940, 358 of the new guns had been completed and by the end of the summer 1940 campaign about 800 had been delivered. Priority for these guns went to the cavalry H39 and it was introduced around tank No. 480. A small number of older H35s were upgraded with the new gun. As in the case of the Renault R35, there was interest in improving the trench-crossing capability of the Hotchkiss, and this led to the design of the tail at Hotchkiss. This was introduced on the production line around tank No. 900 in March 1940. The infantry had two battalions of H35s and six battalions of H39s by May 1940, and a further two separate companies were raised with the final deliveries, totaling about 425 tanks of the roughly 480 on order.

CHAR B

French tank doctrine since the end of World War I envisioned the need for a more powerful tank than the light infantry tanks in order to conduct independent actions. This concept had various names including *char puissant* (powerful tank) and *char de bataille* (battle tank). Development of this tank was unusually protracted, and resulted in a design more suited to 1920 than 1940.

The development of the battle tank can be traced back to one of the main supporters of advanced technology, Gén Edmond Buat, who released a perceptive study in July 1919 outlining future tank needs. Aside from the traditional *char léger* (such as the Renault FT) and the *char lourd* (heavy tank – such as the 2C), Buat saw the need for a *char de combat de l'avenir* (future combat tank). Instead of being designed to deal with enemy infantry, Buat envisioned a future mobile battle where the main opponent would be enemy tanks and armored infantry. The tactical imperative for the *char de bataille*, or "battle tank," was that it would have enough armor to resist enemy field guns of the type encountered in the 1918 fighting, have the firepower to destroy typical defensive field works, have the mobility to surmount trenches and battlefield obstructions, and have the speed to penetrate enemy defenses.

In January 1920, the war ministry set up a commission under Gén Buat to detail the needs for future tanks. Buat cooperated with Gén Jean-Baptiste

The original production batch of Char B tanks served with 511e RCC in the late 1930s. This is "Champagne" (no. 134) built by FCM. In 1940 it was being used for training and did not see combat. (Patton Museum)

The Char B tanks were a popular attraction during the National Day parades on the Champs-Elysées in Paris. This is "Dunkerque" (no. 111), which at the time served with the 511e RCC. In May 1940, it was attached to the newly created 347e CACC and was destroyed near Neuvy sur Loeilly on June 6, 1940. (NARA)

Estienne, the father of the French tank force in World War I, to help define the technical requirements. They sought a new 15-ton tank design that would bridge the gap between the Renault FT light tank and the monstrous FCM 2C breakthrough tank. Estienne proposed a production requirement of a thousand tanks, which provoked considerable industrial interest. In 1921, five French manufacturers offered their concepts. The least adventurous was from Delaunay-Belleville, which resembled nothing more than an enlarged FT tank. Schneider and Renault teamed together to provide a pair of offerings. The SRA (Schneider-Renault A) used a 75mm fortress gun in the hull, while the SRB offered a naval 47mm mle. 02 gun with better antitank performance. Saint-Chamond's FAMH plant also used a short 75mm gun, as did the FCM 21 design. The Delaunay-Belleville design was rejected almost immediately. Of the remaining four designs, all but the SRB encountered prolonged mechanical issues during the 1924 trials. In the end, the SRB was selected as the preferred design, but better features from the other competitors were adapted to the SRB, such as the track from the FCM tank and the suspension design of the Saint-Chamond tank.

Due to cutbacks in defense budgets, the production contracts were pushed off into the indefinite future while the design was refined. One of the most important changes was a decision to increase the armor to 40mm, which boosted the overall weight of the tank from 15 towards 20 tons. Three contracts were issued to Renault, FCM and FAMH on March 18, 1927 to build three pilots of definitive design, now designated as Char de

Bataille B. Trials of the pilot tanks began in 1929 and dragged on for more than five years, since there were simply not enough funds to contemplate production. The aim was to begin production in 1934.

The trials uncovered problems with one of the critical features of the design, the Naeder steering system. This was an advanced servo motor mounted in the powertrain to permit precision steering of the tank in order to aim the gun. Due to the limited space available in the hull front, it was impossible to provide the gun with sufficient traverse. Instead, the driver would aim the gun using the Naeder system. The fragility of the Naeder system prompted FCM to propose the substitution of a Swiss Winterthur hydraulic transmission teamed with a 180hp Sulzer diesel engine. Unfortunately, the Sulzer engine proved to be trouble-prone, and the Char B remained saddled with this dubious steering configuration. One consequence of the problems with the Naeder steering system was to place more emphasis on the turret armament, with the pilots being adapted to mount the ST2 turret from the Char D1 infantry tank. In October 1931, an experimental unit put the pilots through a grueling 225km road march, which emphasized the durability of the design. A production contract for a pre-series batch of seven tanks was planned for 1932 but delayed until 1934. To complicate matters further, the original contracts for the three Char B pilots from the 1926 program had not included development of the turret or armament.

As was the case through so much of the French army, the rise of the Nazi party in Germany in 1933 provided a sudden jolt of reality. The manufacturers set the price at FF2,500,000, but this was negotiated down to FF1,380,000, although the price did not include the guns or turret. After years of delay, the first contract was awarded in March 1934 for seven tanks, followed by a second contract on December 16, 1934 for 20 more. The first batch of tanks was delivered from December 1935 to May 1936, but they were still without their guns or turrets. The ST2 turret was deemed unacceptable since it had frontal armor of only 30mm compared to the 40mm requirement. In the interim, APX developed its new APX-1 turret with the same gun but with heavier armor, and this was selected for both the Char B and the Char D2.

The first unit assigned the Char B was the 511e RCC, reorganized in March 1936 on the basis of the previous heavy tank units responsible for the Mark V* and Char 2C heavy tanks. It eventually had three subordinate battalions, the 9e BCC with the new R35 tank, the 37e BCC with the Char B, and the 51e BCC with the Char 2C. The first section of three Char B tanks did not arrive until the end of September 1937.

CHAR B1 BIS

By the time that the Char B1 had reached production, it was already obsolete. Its 40mm armor was barely adequate to protect it against the new German 37mm antitank gun. The change in designation from Char B to Char B1 in 1934 was part of a new plan to regard the Char B as a family of battle tanks. A scheme from October 1930 involved at least three other proposed versions, the 35 metric ton B2, the 45 metric ton B3 and the 50 metric ton BB. In spite of army interest in the further evolution of this design, Renault was considerably more skeptical about investing its own money in such an outdated design. Instead they proposed the Renault

ACK 1 next generation battle tank, which eventually emerged as the Char G1R. In the event, the urgent need for more battle tanks in the face of German rearmament put an end to the more ambitious evolution of the Char B1 in favor of a "B1 surblindé". This envisioned an increase in the frontal armor to 60mm to protect against the German 37mm antitank gun. The heavier armor led to a redesign of the engine to increase power from 200 to 300hp by adding a second carburetor, but this came at the expense of endurance, which fell from 8 hours to 5 hours between refueling. In the meantime, a new 47mm SA35 tank gun was under development by Puteaux for the S35 cavalry tank, and this was mounted in a modified APX-4 turret for the new version.

Although approved for construction in 1935, the first production contract for the new Char B1 bis was not awarded to Renault until May 1, 1937 due to the continuing delays in the manufacture of the original Char B1. This was for a battalion of 35 tanks at a unit cost of FF1,286,000 without turret and armament, which were to be provided separately by state arsenals. This was followed on October 8, 1937 with a contract for another 35 Char B1 bis. Curiously enough, this 1937 contract rounded out Char B procurement by including funding for a final five Char B1 tanks to complete the equipment of a single battalion. The Char B1 production series was delivered from December 1935 through January 1937. The initial Char B1 bis were delivered from February 1937 and by the time of the war's outbreak on September 1, 1939, a total of 35 Char B1 and 84 Char B1 bis had been delivered and 350 were on order. By the time of the German attack on May 10, 1940, 258 Char B1 bis had been delivered to eight battalions. The tempo of production of the Char B1 bis increased from about seven per month in 1939 to about 32 per month in 1940, and by the end of the campaign 1,178 Char B1 bis had been ordered and 403 completed by Renault, FCM, FAMH, AMX and Schneider.

The definitive Char B1 bis was fitted with the APX-4 turret with the longer 47mm SA35 gun. "Vertus" (no. 372) was delivered to the 41e BCC on November 29, 1939, and is seen here in the spring of 1940 during training. It was commanded by Lt Jacques Hachet of 3/41e BCC. After being separated from the battalion during the confused fighting near Stonne, the tank suffered mechanical problems and was sent back to a rear area repair base in early June 1940. (NARA)

The Char B1 bis was a well-armored and well-armed tank, but suffered from many design flaws that undermined its combat effectiveness. The unusual aiming system for the hull gun was a mistake, since it overburdened the driver. The solution was to redesign the gun mounting to provide a limited amount of traverse for fine aiming. This was to be incorporated on the next version, the Char B1 ter, but this variant was only in prototype stage at the time of the Battle of France. The one-man turret was also a serious mistake, since it obliged the commander to take on the added distractions of loading and aiming the gun. Aside from these inherent design flaws, the tank was plagued with other mechanical issues. Of the 267 known cases of Char B1 bis lost in combat, more than half were abandoned or scuttled by their crews. The Naeder servo motor proved to be a major source of the mechanical problems. Fuel exhaustion was another frequent cause of combat loss. The Char B1 bis had an effective range of 60–90 miles, which was not untypical of tanks of this period. However, the newly formed armored divisions had not yet worked out refueling procedures and in some cases suffered from a shortage of the Lorraine 37L refueling vehicles. At the core of many of the operating problems of the Char B1 bis was the lack of adequate training and crew experience caused by the belated formation of the French armored divisions and the late arrival of the new tanks in the Char B1 bis battalions. More than half of the Char B1 bis tanks deployed in May 1940 had only been delivered 2–4 months before, which restricted the amount of training possible.

Char B1 bis, "Vauquois," (no. 377) of the 41e BCC on exercise in the spring of 1940. During the 1940 fighting it was commanded by Lt Pierre Bourgeois and was knocked out by artillery fire near Perthes on June 10, 1940. (NARA)

Comparative Technical Data: Maneuver Tanks

	D1	D2	B1	B1 bis
Crew	3	3	4	4
Weight: metric tonnes (tons)	14.0 (15.4)	19.7 (21.7)	27.2 (29.9)	31.5 (34.6)
Length: meters (ft)	4.81 (15.8: w/o tail)	5.46 (17.9)	6.35 (20.8)	6.35 (20.8)
Width: meters (ft)	2.16 (7.1)	2.22 (7.3)	2.5 (8.2)	2.5 (8.2)
Height: meters (ft)	2.4 (7.9)	2.66 (8.7)	2.79 (9.2)	2.79 (9.2)
Frontal armor: mm	30	40	40	60
Main gun	47mm SA34	47mm SA34	75mm SA35	75mm SA35
Secondary gun	no	no	47mm SA34	47mm SA35
Machine guns	2 x 7.5mm	2 x 7.5mm	2 x 7.5mm	2 x 7.5mm
Main/secondary gun ammo	112	120	80+50	81+76
Engine (hp)	74	150	250	300
Fuel: liters (gal)	165 (44)	240 (64)	400 (105)	400 (105)
Road speed: km/h (mph)	18.5 (11.5)	23 (14.3)	28 (17.4)	27 (16.8)
Range: km (miles)	90 (56)	100 (62)	200 (124)	180 (112)

Comparative Technical Data: Accompanying Tanks

	R35	R40	H35	H39	FCM36
Crew	2	2	2	2	2
Weight: metric tonnes (tons)	10.6 (11.7)	11.6 (12.7)	10.6 (11.7)	12.1 (13.3)	12.3 (13.5)
Length: meters (ft)	4.02 (13.2)	4.3 (14.1: inc. tail)	4.22 (13.8)	4.22 (13.8 no tail)	4.46 (14.6)
Width: meters (ft)	1.87 (6.1)	2.01 (6.6)	1.85 (6.1)	1.95 (6.4)	2.14 (7.0)
Height: meters (ft)	2.13 (7)	2.15 (7.1)	2.13 (7)	2.13 (7)	2.2 (7.2)
Frontal armor: mm	40	40	40	40	40
Main gun	37mm SA18	37mm SA38	37mm SA18	37mm SA38	37mm SA18
Main gun ammo	100	90	100	100	102
Machine gun	7.5mm	7.5mm	7.5mm	7.5mm	7.5mm
Engine (hp)	82	82	75	120	94
Road speed: km/h (mph)	20 (12.4)	20 (12.4)	28 (17.3)	36.5 (22.7)	24 (14.9)
Fuel: liters (gal)	168 (44)	168 (44)	180 (48)	207 (55)	217 (57)
Range: km (miles)	130 (80)	80 (50)	130 (80)	120 (75)	225 (140)

1: CHAR B1 BIS, 15e BCC, 2e DCR, 1939

The Char B1 bis had some of the most eclectic camouflage schemes, since the tank was produced at five facilities: Renault, FCM, FAMH (Saint-Chamond), AMX (Satory) and Schneider (Atelier du Creusot). Each of the plants tended to have their own interpretation of French camouflage patterns. To add to the mixture, the turret was supplied separately, and the pattern sometimes differed from that of the hull. "Tunisie" (no. 204) displays the second style of Renault factory. This particular tank was built under the October 8, 1936 contract and delivered in mid-1937. The company names for the colors used here were olive green (*vert olive*), beige (*ocre*), sea-green (*vert d'eau*), and dark earth (*terre de Sienne*). This shows "Tunisie" in its gaudy prewar markings. The 15e BCC retained the World War I pattern of markings in 1938 and 1939, with the triangle indicating 3e Companie and the diamond indicating 3e Section; markings were over-painted in 1940.

2: CHAR B1 BIS, 37e BCC, 1ere DCR

"Var," no. 323, was produced under the February 1, 1937 contract by FAMH (Saint-Chamond) and delivered in 1939. By this stage, the French army was shifting towards a more muted camouflage of grey-green (*gris vert*) and dark earth (*terre d'ombre*), and the Saint-Chamond scheme used simple bands of the color. The triangle on the turret rear indicates the 2nd Companie, and the diamond as well as the large S indicates the 3e Section. This letter was often repeated on either side of the hull rear plate.

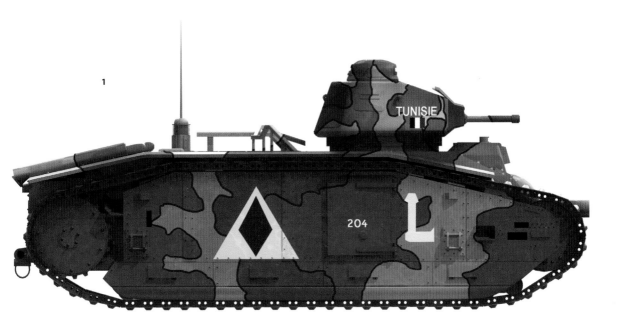

1

2

RENAULT UE INFANTRY VEHICLE

The French army avoided the fad for tankettes that was so popular in European armies in the late 1920s and early 1930s. However, the idea of a small tracked armored vehicle proved to be appealing for other reasons, and the *chenillette* (tankette) became the most widely manufactured French armored vehicle of the 1940 campaign. Although not a tank, the *chenillette* was so important to French army mechanization that it is included here.

The requirement for the *chenillette* stemmed back to the lessons of World War I. In 1922, the French army was mulling over the experience of trench warfare, and concluded that it would be useful to field a vehicle to supply troops in forward trench lines. This had been a difficult and hazardous process between 1915 and 1918, and a tracked armored vehicle seemed to offer a solution, since it could traverse shell-pocked terrain and deliver supplies under enemy machine-gun fire. A requirement emerged in 1930 and was addressed by prototypes from Renault, Citroën and Latil. After tests, the army settled on the Renault "tracteur blindé de ravitaillement d'infanterie type UE" along with accompanying UK tracked trailer. An original tranche of 60 tractors was ordered in October 1931. The design was quite elementary to keep down cost, with an armored hull protecting two crewmen and a stowage box at the rear. The box was automated so that the crew could drive the tractor to the edge of a trench and automatically dump the contents into the trench without leaving the safety of the armored tractor. Power came from a Renault 10CV 38hp motor fitted in the center of the vehicle between the two crewmen. Maximum armor was 9mm, enough to resist machine-gun fire at typical combat ranges. The UE had a range of about 100km at a top road speed of 30km/h. Some thought was given to arming the UE tractor with a machine gun but this was firmly resisted by the infantry branch, which was concerned that armed UEs would be sent off on tank missions instead of their supply mission. However, a total of ten "casemate" UE tankettes with a machine-gun station were built for export to China in the late 1930s.

After the first tranche of 60 Chenillette 1931R was delivered, a second order for 916 followed, which was manufactured from late 1934 to early 1937. These had a variety of improvements including a plate for the triangular towing sign and an extended left side tool bin; the armored domes for the crewmen were also standardized in this series and they were retrofitted to earlier vehicles. The third contract tranche of 220 vehicles made between July and October 1936 had lengthened mudguards. A final fourth tranche of 1,400 vehicles was ordered in 1936, which had the original twin Restor headlights replaced by a single Guicherd armored night-driving light. Due to the size of the fourth order, it was split up between Renault, AMX, Fouga and Berliet, with some minor differences in detail. In total some 2,596 UE tractors were built including UE and UE 2 prototypes, as well as tractors exported to China and Romania.

In 1935, the French army began to contemplate further infantry mechanization and put out a requirement for a successor to the UE tractor. Some five designs were considered and the army proceeded to order designs from Renault, Lorraine and Berliet. Of these, only the Renault infantry tractor was significant, and this was simply a modernized version

This Chenillette UE has the matricule 79154 identifying it as the 43rd production vehicle from 1932. It has the characteristic features of the first production tranche, including the absence of the plate between the crew hatches for the towing marking. (NARA)

of the UE called the Chenillette 1937R UE 2. This introduced a semiautomatic four-speed clutch and transmission. It could be distinguished from the early production tranches by small details such as the use of "U" towing hooks in place of the "pig-tail" hooks on the earlier UE tractors. About 2,300 UE 2 were ordered from three manufacturers through June 1940, including AMX, Berliet, and Fouga. A total of about 4,900 UE and UE 2 tractors were completed by June 1940 of the 6,200 ordered, and perhaps as many as 5,300 were eventually completed, including those finished before and shortly after the 1940 armistice. However, only about 3,300 reached the troops and there were 1,278 in various depots at the time of the armistice. Romania signed a contract in 1937 to manufacture 300 UE tractors under license at the Malaxa plant in Bucharest. Production did not begin until 1939, however, and due to the shortage of parts from France only about 113 were completed, plus 13 more that were received from France for a total of 126.

The Renault UE and UE 2 tractors were used in both normal infantry regiments and motorized infantry regiments. Each infantry regiment had

39

A pair of Chenillette UE 2 tractors on exercise before the war, with M62243 in the lead. The UE 2 can be distinguished from the fourth production tranche of UE tractors by the new U hooks on the front. Other late features were the extended mudguards and Guicherd armored headlight. (NARA)

a supply company and a vehicle company, each with six tractors for a total of 12. The motorized regiments added a support company with two UE tractors in each battalion for a total of 18 tractors per regiment. Each infantry division also had a divisional antitank company equipped with UE tractors towing the standard 25mm SA34 antitank gun. The UE tractors were used in other types of units for other chores including towing fuel trailers, mortars, and other specialized equipment.

G

1: LORRAINE 37L TRC, 510e RCC, AUGUST 1939
The Lorraine tank refueling vehicles were painted in the typical 1939–40 scheme of overall army green or grey-green with a sprayed pattern of dark earth brown. Unit insignia were not particularly common, but this particular transporter carries the regimental insignia of the 510e RCC. This insignia was probably over-painted after the outbreak of the war, when the regiment's battalions (15e and 22e BCC) were mobilized.

2: LORRAINE 38L VBCP, 17e BCP, 2e DCR, MAY 1940
As in the case of the Lorraine tank refueling vehicles, the mechanized infantry vehicles were usually painted in the standard 1939–40 scheme of army green/grey-green with a pattern of dark earth brown. The 17e BCP (2 DCr) used a distinctive system of domino insignia to distinguish subformations. The other battalion equipped with these vehicles, the 5e BCP (1e DCr), used the more traditional playing card insignia. The inset drawing shows the standard French army symbol for "towed load" warning sign in blue with a yellow triangle. On the Lorraine 37L refueling transporter, it was mounted on a special illuminated panel on the engine deck, while on the Lorraine 38L mechanized infantry vehicle it was usually mounted on a detachable sign post that was clipped on the left front corner of the rear superstructure when needed.

1

2

CHENILLETTE LORRAINE

The French army had considered adopting a specialized vehicle for the supply and technical support of tank battalions, but the Citroën Kégresse P17 half-tracks acquired in the early 1930s for the Char D1 battalions proved inadequate. The Renault ACD 1, a tracked unarmored vehicle based on the UE, was ordered in 1936, but there was interest in a fully armored vehicle as well. Specifications for the new tank resupply vehicle (TRC: *tracteur de ravitaillement pour chars*) was released on April 17, 1936. Societé Lorraine de Dietrich had offered its CRI (*chenillette de ravitaillement d'infanterie*) armored tractor for the 1935 infantry requirement, and lengthened it for the TRC bid. The Lorraine 37L TRC had a crew of two and armor up to 9mm thick. In the TRC role, it towed a special tracked VRC fuel trailer carrying 565 liters of fuel. The primary function of the TRC was to refuel the tanks in forward areas, though other supplies could be carried in the rear compartment. The plan was to deploy 12 TRCs in each light tank battalion, 18 in Char B1 bis battalions, and three in each combat squadron of the cavalry's DLM (light mechanized divisions). The Lorraine 37L was selected for the TRC requirement in 1938, and over 450 were on order at the war's outbreak in September 1939, later increased to about 560 by the spring of 1940. The increasing requirements led to plans in 1940 to assemble up to 70 a month from Societé Lorraine and 20–30 from the Fouga plant. At the start of the Battle of France on May 10, 1940, about 450 of the Lorraine 37L TRCs had been delivered and in total about 490 TRCs were produced by the end of the war. Delivery priority went to the armored divisions.

In 1938, plans emerged to equip the mechanized infantry (*chasseurs portés*) of the armored divisions (DCr) with a fully tracked carrier instead of the trucks and half-tracks then in use. The Lorraine 37L emerged as a possible candidate, but the small rear compartment was sufficient for only four troops. As a result, the Lorraine 38L VBCP infantry carrier (*voiture blindée de chasseurs portés*) had a tracked trailer added, which could accommodate six more troops, and the rear compartment was redesigned with armored protection for the troops by raising up the sides. A total of 240 were ordered in September 1939 and a few more than 140 had been delivered by the time of the armistice. They were deployed primarily with the 5e BCP (*bataillon de chasseurs portés*) of the 1e DCr and the 17e BCP of the 2e DCr. A variety of other schemes for the Lorraine tractors were

The basic Lorraine 37L TRC was intended to tow a VRC refueling trailer. (NARA)

underway in 1940, including substantially redesigned infantry carrier, the Lorraine 39L, and tank destroyer armed with the 47mm antitank gun on the Lorraine 37L.

The Lorraine 38L VBCP was an infantry transporter and this shows the prototype along with its associated trailer. The tractor itself had seating for four troops in the rear compartment, while the trailer could accommodate a further six troops. (NARA)

THE SHAPE OF THINGS TO COME

At the time of the Battle of France in May–June 1940, the French army had a broad program of tank modernization underway that would have replaced most of the familiar tank types, including the light infantry tank, the battle tank and the breakthrough tank. Work on a new light tank began at a research office in the AMX plant in response to an October 1937 effort to modernize the existing light tanks. The short-term outcome of this effort was the design of the AMX suspension for the R35 that resulted in the R40. AMX also took heed of an army study favoring the FCM 36 by beginning design of a new light tank that employed the new AMX suspension with a new welded hull design and diesel powerplant influenced by the FCM 36. A *char léger futur* began more formally under tank inspector Gén Keller's program in December 1939. The initial AMX 38 design had 40mm of armor and the same 37mm SA38 gun as contemporary French light tanks. This did not offer enough of a step forward, and a proposed AMX 39 with 48mm armor and a 47mm gun was under deliberation at the time of the Battle of France. Renault was working on a competitive design, the DAC 1, but in the event it did not reach prototype stage.

Development of a new 20-tonne *char moyen d'infanterie* (medium infantry tank) was first broached in a December 1935 infantry department study. This tank was intended to have a hull-mounted 75mm gun and a turret-mounted 47mm like the Char B1 bis, but in a more modern configuration. Seven companies submitted designs for the new Char Moyen G1. The SEAM team under Prince André Poniatowski completed a hull test-bed for their G1P using a modern electric transmission that was completed in late 1937. However, army uncertainty over specifications delayed the program and led to changes such as the switch to a new turret-mounted 75mm gun, and the weight continued to climb towards 30 tonnes. Financial difficulties at SEAM led to a consolidation of its program with that being undertaken by ARL, but the G1P went into limbo after the start of the war in 1939. Renault proposed their futuristic G1R design, known internally as the ACK1, which offered torsion bar suspension, 350hp engine, 60mm cast armor, and a 75mm gun in the turret. The production of the first castings by Schneider was scheduled for July 1940 with the aim of completing the first tank by September 1940. None of the other designs progressed beyond studies. The Renault G1R was being developed in the same time frame as the Soviet T-34 and US M4 Sherman, and would have had similar capabilities had not the armistice ended any further work.

The third major tank program underway in 1940 was a new *char de forteresse* to replace the old Char 2C. This was intended to attack fortified positions such as the German Westwall, but it also had a defensive mission as a gap-filler in the Maginot line. The original November 1936 plan called for a 45-tonne tank with a 75mm gun and 100mm armor. The AMX, ARL and FCM companies made proposals. The army continued to change

A preserved example of the H39 with the later 37mm SA38 gun displayed at the French army's Satory exhibition in the 1990s. This was evidently a tank that had been used by the German army in World War II, as evidenced by the modified cupola with the split hatch. (Author)

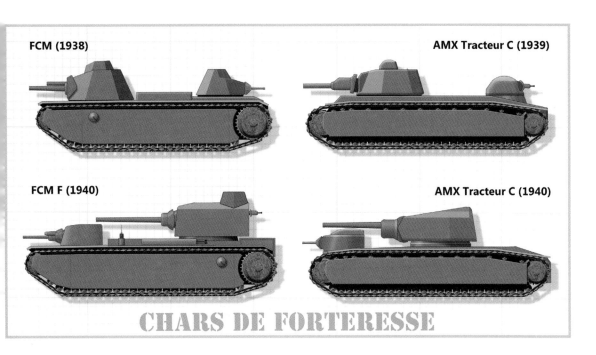

FCM (1938)

AMX Tracteur C (1939)

FCM F (1940)

AMX Tracteur C (1940)

CHARS DE FORTERESSE

the specifications and requirements, leading to a string of design offerings. The earlier configurations tended to follow the Char 2C configuration with the main turret in front and a machine-gun turret in the rear. By 1939–40, the army began to demand more armor and firepower, and this led to schemes for a small subturret in front with an antitank gun or flamethrower and a 90mm gun in the main turret further to the rear. At the end of 1939, the three firms were developing six designs. The project closest to completion was the FCM F1, and the firm presented a full-scale wooden mock-up to the army commission on April 12, 1940. Had it reached production, the FCM F1 would have had 100mm armor, a combat weight of 130 tonnes, a 20km/h road speed, and an armament of a 90mm gun in the main turret and 47mm gun in the subturret.

Design proposals for the Char de forteresse between 1937 and 1940. (Author)

French Infantry Tank Production 1930–40											
Tank	1930	1931	1932	1933	1934	1935	1936	1937	1938	1939	1940	Total
R35							300	245	200	555	311	1,611
FCM36									89	11		100
H35*							100	192	108			400
H39*										374	306	680
D1		10	70	30		50						160
D2							40	10			37	87
B1/ B1bis					3		27	35	25	100	187	377
Total	0	10	70	30	3	50	467	482	422	1,040	841	3,415

*Includes tanks built for the cavalry

Dissatisfaction with the Renault R35 led to a requirement for a future light infantry tank, and AMX completed a single AMX38 pilot shortly before the fall of France. (Pierre Touzin)

FURTHER READING

There has been an upsurge in writing on French tanks of 1940, although there is little in English. François Vauvillier has rejuvenated the old *Histoire et Guerre* magazine, which was renamed starting with no. 74 (Nov–Dec. 2006) as *Guerre, Blindés & Materiél*. It is essential reading for anyone seriously interested in French tanks of the 1940 era. The GBM special issue no. 100 from June 2012, *Tous les blindés de l'armée française*, is especially noteworthy and the most concise single source for French AFVs of the 1920–40 period. The companion magazine, *Tank Zone*, has also had numerous articles on French tanks. These articles are not listed here since they are too numerous. Pascal Danjou's "Trackstory" and "Focus" monographs are also extremely valuable. The "Trackstory" series covers the history of the tanks, while the "Focus" series is oriented towards photographic coverage of preserved museum vehicles, with an eye towards the needs of tank modelers.

Bonnaud, Stéphane, *Chars B au combat: Hommes et materiels du 15ᵉ BCC*, Historie et Collections (2002)

Clarke, Jeffrey, *Military Technology in Republican France: The Evolution of the French Armored Force 1917–40*, UMI (1970)

Danjou, Pascal, *Char B1 bis*, Focus no. 4, Barbotin (2009)

Danjou, Pascal, *Hotchkiss H39*, Focus no. 5, Barbotin (2009)

Danjou, Pascal, *Renault R35*, Focus no. 7, Barbotin (2010)

Danjou, Pascal, *Les Chars B: B1, B1 bis, B1 ter*, Trackstory no. 3, Barbotin (2005)

Danjou, Pascal, *Le Char B1*, Trackstory no. 13, Barbotin (2012)

Danjou, Pascal, *FCM 36*, Trackstory no. 7, Barbotin (2007)

Danjou, Pascal, *Hotchkiss H35/H39*, Trackstory no. 6, Barbotin (2006)

Danjou, Pascal, *Juin 40, L'impossible sursaut*, Trackstory no. 5, Barbotin (2006)

Danjou, Pascal, *Renault D1*, Trackstory no. 8, Barbotin (2008)

Danjou, Pascal, *Renault D2*, Trackstory no. 9, Barbotin (2008)

Danjou, Pascal, *Renault R35/R40*, Trackstory no. 4, Barbotin (2005)

Danjou, Pascal, *Renault FT*, Trackstory no. 10, Barbotin (2009)

Duvignac, André, *Histoire de l'armée motorisée*, Imp. Nationale (1947)

Ferrard, Stéphane, *France 1940: L'armement terrestre*, ETAI (1998)

Hoff, Pierre, *Les programmes d'armament de 1919 à 1939*, SHAT (1982)

Jeudy, Jean-Gabriel, *Chars de France*, ETAI (1997)

Ledwoch, Janusz, *Renault R35 Vol. 1*, Wyd. Militaria (2012)

Ramspacher, E., et al., *Chars et blindés française*, Lavauzelle (1979)

Saint-Martin, Gérard, *L'arme blindée française, Tome 1: Mai–Juin 1940, Les blindés français dans la tourmente*, Economica (1998)

Tirone, Laurent, et al., *Les engins de combat de l'armée française en 1940*, Trucks & Tanks Hors-Serie no. 5, Caraktére (2010)

Touzin, Pierre, *Les engins blindés français 1920–1945*, vol. 1, SERA (1976)

Touzin, Pierre, *Les véhicules blindés français 1900–1944*, EPA (1979)

Vauvillier, François, and Touraine, J. M., *L'automobile sous l'uniforme 1939–40*, Massin (1992)

Voisin, Pierre, *Ceux des chars*, Archat (1941)

Renault recognized that the Char B1 bis was a technical dead end, and began promoting more modern designs for the future battle tank requirement. This is a wooden mock-up of the Char G1R. (Pierre Touzin)

INDEX

References to images are in **bold**. References to plates are in **bold** with captions in brackets.